# A Year
# Celebrations

Nicola Tuxworth

OXFORD
UNIVERSITY PRESS

OXFORD
UNIVERSITY PRESS

Great Clarendon Street, Oxford OX2 6DP

Oxford University Press is a department of the University of Oxford.
It furthers the University's objective of excellence in research, scholarship, and education by publishing worldwide in

Oxford New York

Athens Auckland Bangkok Bogotá Buenos Aires Calcutta
Cape Town Chennai Dar es Salaam Delhi Florence Hong Kong Istanbul
Karachi Kuala Lumpur Madrid Melbourne Mexico City Mumbai
Nairobi Paris São Paulo Singapore Taipei Tokyo Toronto Warsaw

with associated companies in Berlin Ibadan



Published in the United Kingdom
by Oxford University Press



First published 2000



British Library Cataloguing in Publication Data

Data available

ISBN 0 19 915700 6

Available in packs

| | | |
|---|---|---|
| Celebrations | Pack of Six (one of each book) | ISBN 0 19 915703 0 |
| Celebrations | Class Pack (six of each book) | ISBN 0 19 915704 9 |

Printed in Hong Kong

**Acknowledgements**

The Publisher would like to thank the following for permission to reproduce photographs:

Barnaby's Picture Library: p 11 (bottom); J Allan Cash: pp 15 (bottom), 16, 22; Circa Photo Library/William Holtby: p 21 (top); Circa Photo Library/B J Mistry: p 13 (top); Circa Photo Library/Barrie Searle: p 8; Circa Photo Library/John Smith: pp 10 (top), 18, 19 (bottom); Collections/Brian Shuel: p 11 (top); Corbis UK Ltd/David Cummings/Eye Ubiquitous: p 15 (middle); Corbis UK Ltd/Bennett Dean/Eye Ubiquitous: p 10 (bottom); Corbis UK Ltd/Philip Gould: p 6 (right); Corbis UK Ltd/Dave G Houser: p 7 (middle); Corbis UK Ltd/Stephanie Maze: p 6; Corel Professional Photos: title page, pp 7 (top), 24, back cover; Eye Ubiquitous/Tim Page: p 12; Sally & Richard Greenhill: p 5 (middle); The Hutchison Library/Michael Macintyre: p 7 (bottom); The Image Bank: pp 5 (bottom), 9 (bottom); Images of India: p 17 (bottom); Oxford University Press: p 9 (top); Ruth & Bury Peerless: pp 17 (top), 19 (top); The Press Association: pp 14, 15 (top); Martin Sookias: pp 5 (top), 13 (bottom); The Stockmarket: p 23 (top); Superstock: p 23 (bottom); Travel Ink/Luc Janssens: p 4.

Front cover photograph is by Corel Professional Photos.

Illustrations by Tony Morris c/o Linda Rogers Artists.

# Contents



◀▶

On some pages of the book, you will see this symbol. It means that the celebration does not happen at the same time each year.

# Chinese New Year

All over the world, Chinese people celebrate New Year with **feasting** and processions. People pray for good luck for themselves and their families in the year to come.

Chinese New Year celebrations in the Netherlands.

On New Year's Day, huge dragons are paraded through the streets. Drums bang, firecrackers explode, and big crowds gather to join the fun.

People send presents and New Year cards to each other. Sometimes children are given lucky money in special red envelopes.

On New Year's Eve, many Chinese families eat a special meal together.

People get ready for New Year by cleaning and putting up decorations.

# Carnival

Carnival is a happy time of dancing, music and feasting. In many Christian countries it takes place before **Lent** begins. Lent is forty days when people pray and give up certain foods. This is called **fasting**. People **feast** on sweet fatty foods and enjoy themselves for a few days before this solemn time.

Thousands of people watched this carnival parade in Brazil.

Drummers beat out rhythms for whirling dancers at a **Mardi Gras** parade in Guadeloupe.

At the Venice carnival in Italy, people dress up in gorgeous costumes.

Knot-shaped biscuits called pretzels are a special treat at carnival time in Germany.

At many carnivals giant figures are paraded through the streets. This is a **Mardi Gras** parade in Brazil.

# Passover

Passover, or Pesach, is one of the oldest festivals in the world. At Passover, Jewish families say prayers and eat a special meal together (the Seder meal). They remember the time when Moses led their escape from Egypt.

During the Seder meal, the youngest child has to ask questions, starting with, "Why is this night different from any other night?" To answer these questions, adults tell the story of Passover.

Special foods are put on the Seder plate. Each food helps Jewish people remember part of the story of Pesach.

Passover lasts for a week. At the beginning and the end of Passover special prayers are held in the synagogue.

# Baisakhi Day

April 13th is one of the most important days in the Sikh calendar. As well as being the Sikh New Year, Baisakhi Day celebrates the beginning of a special group of Sikhs hundreds of years ago.

Sikh men do not cut their hair. They carry swords to show that they will defend their faith.

The most holy Sikh temple is the Golden Temple at Amritsar, in India. A parade is held here each year to celebrate Baisakhi day.

# May Day

The first day of May has been celebrated for hundreds of years in cool, European countries. The arrival of warmer weather is greeted with dancing, singing, and parades.

In some towns and villages, people choose a May queen to lead the May parade.

Sometimes, children dance around a maypole. They hold coloured ribbons which weave into a pattern.

# Poson Day

Many centuries ago, a monk called Mahinda came to Sri Lanka from India to teach the king of Sri Lanka about the Buddhist faith. Poson Day is a colourful, happy celebration of Mahinda's arrival.

On Poson Day, people visit holy shrines.

# Raksha-bandhan

At the Hindu festival of Raksha-bandhan, sisters tie a silk bracelet around their brothers' wrists to show the love between brothers and sisters.

The bracelet, or rakhi, is tied around a charm to bring good luck.

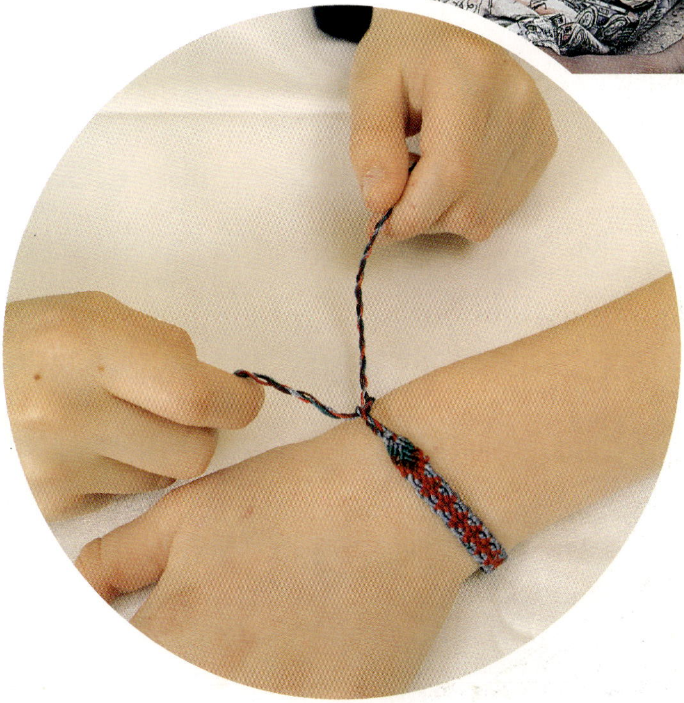

Children around the world make friendship bracelets from coloured thread.

# Notting Hill Carnival

The Notting Hill Carnival in London is three days of music, dancing, and amazing costumes. Thousands of people parade through the streets on huge, decorated floats, and thousands more people turn out to watch.

Carnivals like this one started in the Caribbean islands, hundreds of years ago. When people from the Caribbean moved to Britain, they started a carnival of their own. Caribbean carnivals are held in February, but in Britain, the weather is better in August.

Everyone joins in the fun at carnival time!

The wonderful costumes take months to design and make.

Steel bands are a very important part of the carnival. The drummers make joyful music for the dancers. Steel drums used to be made out of old oil drums.

# Harvest Festivals

Harvest takes place at different times of the year around the world. People give thanks for the harvest of food with prayers and special services. Some people celebrate in churches or temples, others celebrate outside.

A fishing festival takes place in February in Argunagu, a village in the African country of Nigeria. Fishermen stand in the river with their nets and whoever catches the biggest fish wins a prize. A big tent is built on the river bank, and there is music and dancing for two days.

In some Christian churches, children bring food to a special harvest service. Fruit and vegetables are piled high in a colourful display. Later, the food is given away to hospitals and people in need.

This harvest festival takes place in the state of Kerala, India. People celebrate for four days. There are processions, **feasts**, and boat races.

Boat race at Onam harvest festival.

# Diwali

The Hindu festival of Diwali is also celebrated by Sikhs. People light lanterns and candles in their houses and remember the story of the Ramayana, when good won a battle against evil.

Diwali lamps are called divas. Divas welcome Lakshmi, the goddess of prosperity. People hope that Lakshmi will bring them good fortune.

Rama and Sita are the heroes of the Ramayana story. They are sitting on a throne. Many Hindus believe that Rama was crowned king on the day of Diwali.

Lots of dances and parties are held at Diwali. This dance is called the dandia raas. As the music gets faster and faster, everyone dances around their partners and taps their sticks together. You have to be careful not to hit your partner with the stick!

# Thanksgiving

In the United States, nobody has to go to work on Thanksgiving Day. Everyone tries to be with their family and eat a special meal together.

Hundreds of years ago, Dutch and English families came to America in search of freedom. The people who already lived in America showed them how to grow the local food, and how to breed turkeys. Thanksgiving remembers the time when the settlers gave thanks to God for their first harvest.

# Eid ul-Fitr

Eid ul-Fitr is a Muslim celebration held at the end of Ramadan. During the month of Ramadan, Muslims must not eat food between sunrise and sunset. This is called **fasting**. At Eid ul-Fitr, special prayers are said at the mosque, and then people exchange cards and presents and have a feast.

Children often have new clothes for Eid.

At Eid, people send each other cards with beautiful pictures on the front.

# Christmas

On December the 25th, Christians all over the world celebrate the birth of Jesus Christ in Bethlehem. People go to church, give each other presents, decorate their houses, and cook a big meal for friends and family.

In many countries, a fir tree is decorated with lights and tinsel.

Some people collect money by singing special Christmas hymns called carols. The money is given to charity.

# Kwanzaa

Not all festivals are very old. Kwanzaa is a new festival started by African-Americans in the United States. They celebrate the harvest in Africa, and remember the way of life of their African ancestors.

Everyone drinks from a special cup to share the celebration.

Seven candles are lit in a stand called a kinara.

# Glossary

**fasting** To stop eating certain foods or to stop eating for a certain time.

**feasting** To eat lots of rich food.

**Lent** A period of 40 days before Easter when some Christians give up certain foods and spend time praying.

**Mardi Gras** A special carnival held at the beginning of **Lent**.

# Index